On Dreams

DOVER · THRIFT · EDITIONS

On Dreams

SIGMUND FREUD

Translated by M. D. Eder

DOVER PUBLICATIONS, INC.
Mineola, New York

DOVER THRIFT EDITIONS

GENERAL EDITOR: PAUL NEGRI

EDITOR OF THIS VOLUME: SUSAN L. RATTINER

Copyright

Copyright © 2001 by Dover Publications, Inc.
All rights reserved under Pan American and International Copyright Conventions.

Published in Canada by General Publishing Company, Ltd., 30 Lesmill Road, Don Mills, Toronto, Ontario.

Bibliographical Note

This Dover edition, first published in 2001, contains the unabridged text of M. D. Eder's "authorised" English translation from the second German edition (1911) of *On Dreams*, originally published by William Heinemann, London, in 1914. A new introductory Note has been specially prepared for the present edition.

Library of Congress Cataloging-in-Publication Data

Freud, Sigmund, 1856–1939.
    [Über den Traum. English]
    On dreams / Sigmund Freud ; translated by M.D. Eder.
        p. cm. — (Dover thrift editions)
    Originally published: London : Heinemann, 1914. With new introd.
    ISBN 0-486-41595-3 (pbk.)
    1. Dreams. I. Eder, M. D. (Montague David), 1866–1936. II. Title. III. Series.

BF1078 .F77313 2001
154.6'3—dc21

                                                                00-065776

Manufactured in the United States of America
Dover Publications, Inc., 31 East 2nd Street, Mineola, N.Y. 11501

Note

SIGMUND FREUD (1856–1939) was raised in Vienna, Austria, and attended the University of Vienna at the age of seventeen. He studied neuroanatomy there, and became a lecturer in neuropathology in 1885. A brilliant researcher, he formulated groundbreaking theories on the workings of the human psyche. Freud's ideas about human behavior, central to the development of psychoanalysis and psychotherapy in the twentieth century, often focused on the role of the unconscious mind in our lives and the irrational impulses that spring from it.

In Freud's view, dreams are the principal key to the unconscious mind, and he perceived the dream process as a form of regression to a more primitive stage of development. His first book on the topic, *The Interpretation of Dreams*, was published in 1899. It was such a lengthy and formidable work that Freud decided to write a more accessible version entitled *On Dreams*. First published in 1901, this brief work reiterated his theory of the dream (the so-called "dream work") as distorted wish fulfillment. Freud also asserted that familiarity with the dreamer's personal history afforded the analyst a distinct advantage—the ability to discern subconscious wishes as well as any underlying symbolism.

Contents

I.

In what we may term "prescientific days" people were in no uncertainty about the interpretation of dreams. When they were recalled after awakening they were regarded as either the friendly or hostile manifestation of some higher powers, demoniacal and Divine. With the rise of scientific thought the whole of this expressive mythology was transferred to psychology; to-day there is but a small minority among educated persons who doubt that the dream is the dreamer's own psychical act.

But since the downfall of the mythological hypothesis an interpretation of the dream has been wanting. The conditions of its origin; its relationship to our psychical life when we are awake; its independence of disturbances which, during the state of sleep, seem to compel notice; its many peculiarities repugnant to our waking thought; the incongruence between its images and the feelings they engender; then the dream's evanescence, the way in which, on awakening, our thoughts thrust it aside as something bizarre, and our reminiscences mutilating or rejecting it—all these and many other problems have for many hundred years demanded answers which up till now could never have been satisfactory. Before all there is the question as to the meaning of the dream, a question which is in itself double-sided. There is, firstly, the psychical significance of the dream, its position with regard to the psychical processes, as to a possible biological function; secondly, has the dream a meaning—can sense be made of each single dream as of other mental syntheses?

Three tendencies can be observed in the estimation of dreams. Many philosophers have given currency to one of these tendencies, one which at the same time preserves something of the dream's former over-valuation. The foundation of dream life is for them a peculiar

1

state of psychical activity, which they even celebrate as elevation to some higher state. Schubert, for instance, claims: "The dream is the liberation of the spirit from the pressure of external nature, a detachment of the soul from the fetters of matter." Not all go so far as this, but many maintain that dreams have their origin in real spiritual excitations, and are the outward manifestations of spiritual powers whose free movements have been hampered during the day ("Dream Phantasies," Scherner, Volkelt). A large number of observers acknowledge that dream life is capable of extraordinary achievements—at any rate, in certain fields ("Memory").

In striking contradiction with this the majority of medical writers hardly admit that the dream is a psychical phenomenon at all. According to them dreams are provoked and initiated exclusively by stimuli proceeding from the senses or the body, which either reach the sleeper from without or are accidental disturbances of his internal organs. The dream has no greater claim to meaning and importance than the sound called forth by the ten fingers of a person quite unacquainted with music running his fingers over the keys of an instrument. The dream is to be regarded, says Binz, "as a physical process always useless, frequently morbid." All the peculiarities of dream life are explicable as the incoherent effort, due to some physiological stimulus, of certain organs, or of the cortical elements of a brain otherwise asleep.

But slightly affected by scientific opinion and untroubled as to the origin of dreams, the popular view holds firmly to the belief that dreams really have got a meaning, in some way they do foretell the future, whilst the meaning can be unravelled in some way or other from its oft bizarre and enigmatical content. The reading of dreams consists in replacing the events of the dream, so far as remembered, by other events. This is done either scene by scene, *according to some rigid key*, or the dream as a whole is replaced by something else of which it was a *symbol*. Serious-minded persons laugh at these efforts—"Dreams are but sea-foam!"

II.

ONE DAY I discovered to my amazement that the popular view grounded in superstition, and not the medical one, comes nearer to the truth about dreams. I arrived at new conclusions about dreams by the use of a new method of psychological investigation, one which had rendered me good service in the investigation of phobias, obsessions, illusions, and the like, and which, under the name "psycho-analysis," had found acceptance by a whole school of investigators. The manifold analogies of dream life with the most diverse conditions of psychical disease in the waking state have been rightly insisted upon by a number of medical observers. It seemed, therefore, *a priori*, hopeful to apply to the interpretation of dreams methods of investigation which had been tested in psychopathological processes. Obsessions and those peculiar sensations of haunting dread remain as strange to normal consciousness as do dreams to our waking consciousness; their origin is as unknown to consciousness as is that of dreams. It was practical ends that impelled us, in these diseases, to fathom their origin and formation. Experience had shown us that a cure and a consequent mastery of the obsessing ideas did result when once those thoughts, the connecting links between the morbid ideas and the rest of the psychical content, were revealed which were heretofore veiled from consciousness. The procedure I employed for the interpretation of dreams thus arose from psychotherapy.

This procedure is readily described, although its practice demands instruction and experience. Suppose the patient is suffering from intense morbid dread. He is requested to direct his attention to the idea in question, without, however, as he has so frequently done, meditating upon it. Every impression about it, without any exception, which occurs to him should be imparted to the doctor. The statement which will be perhaps then made, that he cannot concentrate his attention upon anything at all, is to be countered by assuring him most positively that such a blank state of mind is utterly impossible. As a matter of fact, a great number of impressions will soon occur, with which others will associate themselves. These will be invariably accompanied by the expression of the observer's opinion that they have no meaning or are unimportant. It will be at once noticed that it is this self-criticism which prevented the patient from imparting the ideas, which had indeed already excluded them from consciousness. If the patient can be induced to abandon this self-criticism and to pursue the trains of thought which are yielded by concentrating the attention, most significant matter will be obtained, matter which will be presently seen to be clearly linked to the morbid idea in question. Its connection with other ideas will be manifest, and later on will permit the replacement of the morbid idea by a fresh one, which is perfectly adapted to psychical continuity.

This is not the place to examine thoroughly the hypothesis upon which this experiment rests, or the deductions which follow from its invariable success. It must suffice to state that we obtain matter enough for the resolution of every morbid idea if we especially direct our attention to the *unbidden* associations *which disturb our thoughts*—those which are otherwise put aside by the critic as worthless refuse. If the procedure is exercised on oneself, the best plan of helping the experiment is to write down all one's first indistinct fancies.

I will now point out where this method leads when I apply it to the examination of dreams. Any dream could be made use of in this way. From certain motives I, however, choose a dream of my own, which appears confused and meaningless to my memory, and one which has the advantage of brevity. Probably my dream of last night satisfies the requirements. Its content, fixed immediately after awakening, runs as follows:

"*Company; at table or table d'hôte. . . . Spinach is served. Mrs. E. L., sitting next to me, gives me her undivided attention, and places her hand familiarly upon my knee. In defence I remove her hand. Then she says: 'But you have always had such beautiful eyes.' . . . I then distinctly see something like two eyes as a sketch or as the contour of a spectacle lens. . . .*"

This is the whole dream, or, at all events, all that I can remember. It appears to me not only obscure and meaningless, but more especially odd. Mrs. E. L. is a person with whom I am scarcely on visiting terms, nor to my knowledge have I ever desired any more cordial relationship. I have not seen her for a long time, and do not think there was any mention of her recently. No emotion whatever accompanied the dream process.

Reflecting upon this dream does not make it a bit clearer to my mind. I will now, however, present the ideas, without premeditation and without criticism, which introspection yielded. I soon notice that it is an advantage to break up the dream into its elements, and to search out the ideas which link themselves to each fragment.

Company; at table or table d'hôte. The recollection of the slight event with which the evening of yesterday ended is at once called up. I left a small party in the company of a friend, who offered to drive me home in his cab. "I prefer a taxi," he said; "that gives one such a pleasant occupation; there is always something to look at." When we were in the cab, and the cab-driver turned the disc so that the first sixty hellers were visible, I continued the jest. "We have hardly got in and we already owe sixty hellers. The taxi always reminds me of the table d'hôte. It makes me avaricious and selfish by continuously reminding me of my debt. It seems to me to mount up too quickly, and I am always afraid that I shall be at a disadvantage, just as I cannot resist at table d'hôte the comical fear that I am getting too little, that I must look after myself." In farfetched connection with this I quote:

> "To earth, this weary earth, ye bring us,
> To guilt ye let us heedless go."

Another idea about the table d'hôte. A few weeks ago I was very cross with my dear wife at the dinner-table at a Tyrolese health resort, because she was not sufficiently reserved with some neighbours with whom I wished to have absolutely nothing to do. I begged her to occupy herself rather with me than with the strangers. That is just as if I had *been at a disadvantage at the table d'hôte.* The contrast between the behaviour of my wife at that table and that of Mrs. E. L. in the dream now strikes me: "*Addresses herself entirely to me.*"

Further, I now notice that the dream is the reproduction of a little scene which transpired between my wife and myself when I was secretly courting her. The caressing under cover of the tablecloth was an answer to a wooer's passionate letter. In the dream, however, my wife is replaced by the unfamiliar E. L.

Mrs. E. L. is the daughter of a man to whom I *owed money!* I cannot help noticing that here there is revealed an unsuspected connection between the dream content and my thoughts. If the chain of associations be followed up which proceeds from one element of the dream one is soon led back to another of its elements. The thoughts evoked by the dream stir up associations which were not noticeable in the dream itself.

Is it not customary, when someone expects others to look after his interests without any advantage to themselves, to ask the innocent question satirically: "Do you think this will be done *for the sake of your beautiful eyes?*" Hence Mrs. E. L.'s speech in the dream. "You have always had such beautiful eyes," means nothing but "people always do everything to you for love of you; you have had *everything for nothing.*" The contrary is, of course, the truth; I have always paid dearly for whatever kindness others have shown me. Still, the fact that I *had a ride for nothing* yesterday when my friend drove me home in his cab must have made an impression upon me.

In any case, the friend whose guests we were yesterday has often made me his debtor. Recently I allowed an opportunity of requiting him to go by. He has had only one present from me, an antique shawl, upon which eyes are painted all round, a so-called Occhiale, as a *charm* against the *Malocchio*. Moreover, he is an *eye specialist*. That same evening I had asked him after a patient whom I had sent to him for *glasses*.

As I remarked, nearly all parts of the dream have been brought into new connection. I still might ask why in the dream it was *spinach* that was served up. Because spinach called up a little scene which recently occurred at our table. A child, whose *beautiful eyes* are really deserving of praise, refused to eat spinach. As a child I was just the same; for a long time I loathed *spinach*, until in late life my tastes altered, and it became one of my favourite dishes. The mention of this dish brings my own childhood and that of my child's near together. "You should be glad that you have some spinach," his mother had said to the little gourmet. "Some children would be very glad to get spinach." Thus I am reminded of the parents' duties towards their children. Goethe's words—

> "To earth, this weary earth, ye bring us,
> To guilt ye let us heedless go"—

take on another meaning in this connection.

Here I will stop in order that I may recapitulate the results of the analysis of the dream. By following the associations which were linked to the single elements of the dream torn from their context, I have been led to a series of thoughts and reminiscences where I am bound to recognise interesting expressions of my psychical life. The matter yielded by an analysis of the dream stands in intimate relationship with the dream content, but this relationship is so special that I should never have been able to have inferred the new discoveries directly from the dream itself. The dream was passionless, disconnected, and unintelligible. During the time that I am unfolding the thoughts at the back of the dream I feel intense and well-grounded emotions. The thoughts themselves fit beautifully together into chains logically bound together with certain central ideas which ever repeat themselves. Such ideas not represented in the dream itself are in this instance the antitheses *selfish, unselfish, to be indebted, to work for nothing*. I could draw closer the threads of the web which analysis has disclosed, and would then be able to show how they all run together into a single knot; I am debarred from making this work public by considerations of a private, not of a scientific, nature. After having cleared up many things which I do not willingly acknowledge as mine, I should have much to reveal which had better remain my secret. Why, then, do not I choose another dream whose analysis would be more suitable for publication, so that I could awaken a fairer conviction of the sense and cohesion of the results disclosed by analysis? The answer is, because every dream which I investigate leads to the same difficulties and places me under the same need of discretion; nor should I forgo this difficulty any the more were I to analyse the dream of someone else. That could only be done when opportunity allowed all concealment to be dropped without injury to those who trusted me.

The conclusion which is now forced upon me is that the dream is a *sort of substitution* for those emotional and intellectual trains of thought which I attained after complete analysis. I do not yet know the process by which the dream arose from those thoughts, but I perceive that it is wrong to regard the dream as psychically unimportant, a purely physical process which has arisen from the activity of isolated cortical elements awakened out of sleep.

I must further remark that the dream is far shorter than the thoughts which I hold it replaces; whilst analysis discovered that the dream was provoked by an unimportant occurrence the evening before the dream.

Naturally, I would not draw such far-reaching conclusions if only one analysis were know to me. Experience has shown me that when the associations of any dream are honestly followed such a chain of thought is revealed, the constituent parts of the dream reappear correctly and sensibly linked together; the slight suspicion that this concatenation was merely an accident of a single first observation must, therefore, be absolutely relinquished. I regard it, therefore, as my right to establish this new view by a proper nomenclature. I contrast the dream which my memory evokes with the dream and other added matter revealed by analysis: the former I call the dream's *manifest content*; the latter, without at first further subdivision, its *latent content*. I arrive at two new problems hitherto unformulated: (1) What is the psychical process which has transformed the latent content of the dream into its manifest content? (2) What is the motive or the motives which have made such transformation exigent. The process by which the change from latent to manifest content is executed I name the *dream work*. In contrast with this is the *work of analysis*, which produces the reverse transformation. The other problems of the dream—the inquiry as to its stimuli, as to the source of its materials, as to its possible purpose, the function of dreaming, the forgetting of dreams—these I will discuss in connection with the latent dream content.

I shall take every care to avoid a confusion between the *manifest* and the *latent content*, for I ascribe all the contradictory as well as the incorrect accounts of dream-life to the ignorance of this latent content, now first laid bare through analysis.

III.

THE CONVERSION of the latent dream thoughts into those manifest deserves our close study as the first known example of the transformation of psychical stuff from one mode of expression into another. From a mode of expression which, moreover, is readily intelligible into another which we can only penetrate by effort and with guidance, although this new mode must be equally reckoned as an effort of our own psychical activity. From the standpoint of the relationship of latent to manifest dream content, dreams can be divided into three classes. We can, in the first place, distinguish those dreams which have a *meaning* and are, at the same time, *intelligible*, which allow us to penetrate into our psychical life without further ado. Such dreams are numerous; they are usually short, and, as a general rule, do not seem very noticeable, because everything remarkable or exciting surprise is absent. Their occurrence is, moreover, a strong argument against the doctrine which derives the dream from the isolated activity of certain cortical elements. All signs of a lowered or subdivided psychical activity are wanting. Yet we never raise any objection to characterising them as dreams, nor do we confound them with the products of our waking life.

A second group is formed by those dreams which are indeed self-coherent and have a distinct meaning, but appear strange because we are unable to reconcile their meaning with our mental life. That is the case when we dream, for instance, that some dear relative has died of plague when we know of no ground for expecting, apprehending, or assuming anything of the sort; we can only ask ourself wonderingly: "What brought that into my head?" To the third group those dreams belong which are void of both meaning and intelligibility; they are *incoherent, complicated, and meaningless*. The overwhelming number of our dreams partake of this character, and this has given rise to the

9

contemptuous attitude towards dreams and the medical theory of their limited psychical activity. It is especially in the longer and more complicated dream-plots that signs of incoherence are seldom missing.

The contrast between manifest and latent dream-content is clearly only of value for the dreams of the second and more especially for those of the third class. Here are problems which are only solved when the manifest dream is replaced by its latent content; it was an example of this kind, a complicated and unintelligible dream, that we subjected to analysis. Against our expectation we, however, struck upon reasons which prevented a complete cognizance of the latent dream thought. On the repetition of this same experience we were forced to the supposition that there is an *intimate bond, with laws of its own, between the unintelligible and complicated nature of the dream and the difficulties attending communication of the thoughts connected with the dream.* Before investigating the nature of this bond, it will be advantageous to turn our attention to the more readily intelligible dreams of the first class where, the manifest and latent content being identical, the dream work seems to be omitted.

The investigation of these dreams is also advisable from another standpoint. The dreams of *children* are of this nature; they have a meaning, and are not bizarre. This, by the way, is a further objection to reducing dreams to a dissociation of cerebral activity in sleep, for why should such a lowering of psychical functions belong to the nature of sleep in adults, but not in children? We are, however, fully justified in expecting that the explanation of psychical processes in children, essentially simplified as they may be, should serve as an indispensable preparation towards the psychology of the adult.

I shall therefore cite some examples of dreams which I have gathered from children. A girl of nineteen months was made to go without food for a day because she had been sick in the morning, and, according to nurse, had made herself ill through eating strawberries. During the night, after a day of fasting, she was heard calling out her name during sleep, and adding: *"Tawberry, eggs, pap."* She is dreaming that she is eating, and selects out of her menu exactly what she supposes she will not get much of just now.

The same kind of dream about a forbidden dish was that of a little boy of twenty-two months. The day before he was told to offer his uncle a present of a small basket of cherries, of which the child was, of course, only allowed one to taste. He woke up with the joyful news: "Hermann eaten up all the cherries."

A girl of three and a half years had made during the day a sea trip which was too short for her, and she cried when she had to get out of the boat. The next morning her story was that during the night she had been on the sea, thus continuing the interrupted trip.

A boy of five and a half years was not at all pleased with his party during a walk in the Dachstein region. Whenever a new peak came into sight he asked if that were the Dachstein, and, finally, refused to accompany the party to the waterfall. His behaviour was ascribed to fatigue; but a better explanation was forthcoming when the next morning he told his dream: *he had ascended the Dachstein*. Obviously he expected the ascent of the Dachstein to be the object of the excursion, and was vexed by not getting a glimpse of the mountain. The dream gave him what the day had withheld. The dream of a girl of six was similar; her father had cut short the walk before reaching the promised objective on account of the lateness of the hour. On the way back she noticed a signpost giving the name of another place for excursions; her father promised to take her there also some other day. She greeted her father next day with the news that she had dreamt that *her father had been with her to both places*.

What is common in all these dreams is obvious. They completely satisfy wishes excited during the day which remain unrealised. They are simply and undisguisedly realisations of wishes.

The following child-dream, not quite understandable at first sight, is nothing else than a wish realised. On account of poliomyelitis a girl, not quite four years of age, was brought from the country into town, and remained over night with a childless aunt in a big—for her, naturally, huge—bed. The next morning she stated that she had dreamt that *the bed was much too small for her, so that she could find no place in it*. To explain this dream as a wish is easy when we remember that to be "big" is a frequently expressed wish of all children. The bigness of the bed reminded Miss Little-Would-be-Big only too forcibly of her smallness. This nasty situation became righted in her dream, and she grew so big that the bed now became too small for her.

Even when children's dreams are complicated and polished, their comprehension as a realisation of desire is fairly evident. A boy of eight dreamt that he was driven with Achilles in a war-chariot, guided by Diomedes. The day before he was assiduously reading about great heroes. It is easy to show that he took these heroes as his models, and regretted that he was not living in those days.

From this short collection a further characteristic of the dreams of children is manifest—*their connection with the life of the day*. The desires which are realised in these dreams are left over from the day or, as a rule, the day previous, and the feeling has become intently emphasised and fixed during the day thoughts. Accidental and indifferent matters, or what must appear so to the child, find no acceptance in the contents of the dream.

Innumerable instances of such dreams of the infantile type can be found among adults also, but, as mentioned, these are mostly exactly like the manifest content. Thus, a random selection of persons will generally respond to thirst at night-time with a dream about drinking, thus striving to get rid of the sensation and to let sleep continue. Many persons frequently have these comforting *dreams* before waking, just when they are called. They then dream that they are already up, that they are washing, or already in school, at the office, etc., where they ought to be at a given time. The night before an intended journey one not infrequently dreams that one has already arrived at the destination; before going to a play or to a party the dream not infrequently anticipates, in impatience, as it were, the expected pleasure. At other times the dream expresses the realisation of the desire somewhat indirectly; some connection, some sequel must be known—the first step towards recognising the desire. Thus, when a husband related to me the dream of his young wife, that her monthly period had begun, I had to bethink myself that the young wife would have expected a pregnancy if the period had been absent. The dream is then a sign of pregnancy. Its meaning is that it shows the wish realised that pregnancy should not occur just yet. Under unusual and extreme circumstances, these dreams of the infantile type become very frequent. The leader of a polar expedition tells us, for instance, that during the wintering amid the ice the crew, with their monotonous diet and slight rations, dreamt regularly, like children, of fine meals, of mountains of tobacco, and of home.

It is not uncommon that out of some long, complicated and intricate dream one specially lucid part stands out containing unmistakably the realisation of a desire, but bound up with much unintelligible matter. On more frequently analysing the seemingly more transparent dreams of adults, it is astonishing to discover that these are rarely as simple as the dreams of children, and that they cover another meaning beyond that of the realisation of a wish.

It would certainly be a simple and convenient solution of the riddle if the work of analysis made it at all possible for us to trace the meaningless and intricate dreams of adults back to the infantile type, to the realisation of some intensely experienced desire of the day. But there is no warrant for such an expectation. Their dreams are generally full of the most indifferent and bizarre matter, and no trace of the realisation of the wish is to be found in their content.

Before leaving these infantile dreams, which are obviously unrealised desires, we must not fail to mention another chief characteristic of dreams, one that has been long noticed, and one which stands out most clearly in this class. I can replace any of these dreams by a phrase expressing a desire. If the sea trip had only lasted longer; if I were only washed and dressed; if I had only been allowed to keep the cherries instead of giving them to my uncle. But the dream gives something more than the choice, for here the desire is already realised; its realisation is real and actual. The dream presentations consist chiefly, if not wholly, of scenes and mainly of visual sense images. Hence a kind of transformation is not entirely absent in this class of dreams, and this may be fairly designated as the dream work. *An idea merely existing in the region of possibility is replaced by a vision of its accomplishment.*

IV.

WE ARE compelled to assume that such transformation of scene has also taken place in intricate dreams, though we do not know whether it has encountered any possible desire. The dream instanced at the commencement, which we analysed somewhat thoroughly, did give us occasion in two places to suspect something of the kind. Analysis brought out that my wife was occupied with others at table, and that I did not like it; in the dream itself *exactly the opposite* occurs, for the person who replaces my wife gives me her undivided attention. But can one wish for anything pleasanter after a disagreeable incident than that the exact contrary should have occurred, just as the dream has it? The stinging thought in the analysis, that I have never had anything for nothing, is similarly connected with the woman's remark in the dream: "You have always had such beautiful eyes." Some portion of the opposition between the latent and manifest content of the dream must be therefore derived from the realisation of a wish.

Another manifestation of the dream work which all incoherent dreams have in common is still more noticeable. Choose any instance, and compare the number of separate elements in it, or the extent of the dream, if written down, with the dream thoughts yielded by analysis, and of which but a trace can be refound in the dream itself. There can be no doubt that the dream working has resulted in an extraordinary compression or *condensation*. It is not at first easy to form an opinion as to the extent of the condensation; the more deeply you go into the analysis, the more deeply you are impressed by it. There will be found no factor in the dream whence the chains of associations do not lead in two or more directions, no scene which has not been pieced together out of two or more impressions and events. For instance, I once dreamt about a kind of swimming-bath where the bathers suddenly separated in all directions; at one place on the edge a person stood bending towards one of the bathers as if to drag him out. The scene was a composite one, made up out of an event that occurred at the time of puberty, and of two pictures, one of which I had seen just shortly before the dream. The two pictures were The Surprise in the Bath, from Schwind's Cycle of the Melusine (note the bathers suddenly separating), and a picture of The Flood, by an Italian master. The little incident was that I once witnessed a lady, who had tarried in the swimming-bath until the men's hour, being helped out of the water by the swimming-master. The scene in the dream which was selected for analysis led to a whole group of reminiscences, each one of which had contributed to the dream content. First of all came the little episode from the time of my courting, of which I have already spoken; the pressure of a hand under the table gave rise in the dream to the "under the table," which I had subsequently to find a place for in my recollection. There was, of course, at the time not a word about "undivided attention." Analysis taught me that this factor is the realisation of a desire through its contradictory and related to the behaviour of my wife at the table d'hôte. An exactly similar and much more important episode of our courtship, one which separated us for an entire day, lies hidden behind this recent recollection. The intimacy, the hand resting upon the knee, refers to a quite different connection and to quite other persons. This element in the dream becomes again the starting-point of two distinct series of reminiscences, and so on.

The stuff of the dream thoughts which has been accumulated for the formation of the dream scene must be naturally fit for this appreciation. There must be one or more common factors. The dream work proceeds like Francis Galton with his family photographs. The different elements are put one on top of the other; what is common to the composite picture stands out clearly, the opposing details cancel each other. This process of reproduction partly explains the wavering statements, of a peculiar vagueness, in so many elements of the dream. For the interpretation of dreams this rule holds good: When analysis discloses *uncertainty* as to *either—or* read *and*, taking each section of the apparent alternatives as a separate outlet for a series of impressions.

When there is nothing in common between the dream thoughts, the dream work takes the trouble to create a something, in order to make a common presentation feasible in the dream. The simplest way to approximate two dream thoughts, which have as yet nothing in common, consists in making such a change in the actual expression of one idea as will meet a slight responsive recasting in the form of the other idea. The process is analogous to that of rhyme, when consonance supplies the desired common factor. A good deal of the dream work consists in the creation of those frequently very witty, but often exaggerated, digressions. These vary from the common presentation in the dream content to dream thoughts which are as varied as are the causes in form and essence which give rise to them. In the analysis of our example of a dream, I find a like case of the transformation of a thought in order that it might agree with another essentially foreign one. In following out the analysis I struck upon the thought: *I should like to have something for nothing.* But this formula is not serviceable to the dream. Hence it is replaced by another one: "I should like to enjoy something free of cost."* The word "kost" (taste), with its double meaning, is appropriate to a table d'hôte; it, moreover, is in place through the special sense in the dream. At home if there is a dish which the children decline, their mother first tries gentle persuasion, with a "Just taste it." That the dream work should unhesitatingly use the double meaning of the word is certainly remarkable; ample experience has shown, however, that the occurrence is quite usual.

Through condensation of the dream certain constituent parts of its content are explicable which are peculiar to the dream life alone, and which are not found in the waking state. Such are the composite and mixed persons, the extraordinary mixed figures, creations comparable with the fantastic animal compositions of Orientals; a moment's thought and these are reduced to unity, whilst the fancies of the dream are ever formed anew in an inexhaustible profusion. Everyone knows such images in his own dreams; manifold are their origins. I can build up a person by borrowing one feature from one person and one from another, or by giving to the form of one the name of another in my dream. I can also visualise one person, but place him in a position which has occurred to another. There is a meaning in all these cases when different persons are amalgamated into one substitute. Such cases denote an "and," a "just like," a comparison of the original person from a certain point of view, a comparison which can be also realised in the dream itself. As a rule, however, the identity of the blended persons is only discoverable by analysis, and is only indicated in the dream content by the formation of the "combined" person.

The same diversity in their ways of formation and the same rules for its solution hold good also for the innumerable medley of dream contents, examples of which I need scarcely adduce. Their strangeness quite disappears when we resolve not to place them on a level with the

---

*"Ich möchte gerne etwas geniessen ohne 'Kosten' zu haben." A pun upon the word "kosten," which has two meanings — "taste" and "cost." In "Die Traumdeutung," third edition, p. 71 footnote, Professor Freud remarks that "the finest example of dream interpretation left us by the ancients is based upon a pun" (from "The Interpretation of Dreams," by Artemidorus Daldianus). "Moreover, dreams are so intimately bound up with language that Ferenczi truly points out that every tongue has its own language of dreams. A dream is as a rule untranslatable into other languages." — TRANSLATOR.

objects of perception as known to us when awake, but to remember that they represent the art of dream condensation by an exclusion of unnecessary detail. Prominence is given to the common character of the combination. Analysis must also generally supply the common features. The dream says simply: *All these things have an "x" in common.* The decomposition of these mixed images by analysis is often the quickest way to an interpretation of the dream. Thus I once dreamt that I was sitting with one of my former university tutors on a bench, which was undergoing a rapid continuous movement amidst other benches. This was a combination of lecture-room and moving staircase. I will not pursue the further result of the thought. Another time I was sitting in a carriage, and on my lap an object in shape like a top-hat, which, however, was made of transparent glass. The scene at once brought to my mind the proverb: "He who keeps his hat in his hand will travel safely through the land." By a slight turn the *glass hat* reminded me of *Auer's light*, and I knew that I was about to invent something which was to make me as rich and independent as his invention had made my countryman, Dr. Auer, of Welsbach; then I should be able to travel instead of remaining in Vienna. In the dream I was travelling with my invention, with the, it is true, rather awkward glass top-hat. The dream work is peculiarly adept at representing two contradictory conceptions by means of the same mixed image. Thus, for instance, a woman dreamt of herself carrying a tall flower-stalk, as in the picture of the Annunciation (Chastity-Mary is her own name), but the stalk was bedecked with thick white blossoms resembling camellias (contrast with chastity: La dame aux Camelias).

A great deal of what we have called "dream condensation" can be thus formulated. Each one of the elements of the dream content is *overdetermined* by the matter of the dream thoughts; it is not derived from one element of these thoughts, but from a whole series. These are not necessarily interconnected in any way, but may belong to the most diverse spheres of thought. The dream element truly represents all this disparate matter in the dream content. Analysis, moreover, discloses another side of the relationship between dream content and dream thoughts. Just as one element of the dream leads to associations with several dream thoughts, so, as a rule, the *one dream thought represents more than one dream element.* The threads of the association do not simply converge from the dream thoughts to the dream content, but on the way they overlap and interweave in every way.

Next to the transformation of one thought in the scene (its "dramatisation"), condensation is the most important and most characteristic feature of the dream work. We have as yet no clue as to the motive calling for such compression of the content.

V.

IN THE complicated and intricate dreams with which we are now concerned, condensation and dramatisation do not wholly account for the difference between dream contents and dream thoughts. There is evidence of a third factor, which deserves careful consideration.

When I have arrived at an understanding of the dream thoughts by my analysis I notice, above all, that the matter of the manifest is very different from that of the latent dream content. That is, I admit, only an apparent difference which vanishes on closer investigation, for in the end I find the whole dream content carried out in the dream thoughts, nearly all the dream thoughts again represented in the dream content. Nevertheless, there does remain a certain amount of difference.

The essential content which stood out clearly and broadly in the dream must, after analysis, rest satisfied with a very subordinate rôle among the dream thoughts. These very dream thoughts which, going by my feelings, have a claim to the greatest importance are either not present at all in the dream content, or are represented by some remote allusion in some obscure region of the dream. I can thus describe these phenomena: *During the dream work the psychical intensity of those thoughts and conceptions to which it properly pertains flows to others which, in my judgment, have no claim to such emphasis.* There is no other process which contributes so much to concealment of the dream's meaning and to make the connection between the dream content and dream ideas irrecognisable. During this process, which I will call *the dream displacement,* I notice also the psychical intensity, significance, or emotional nature of the thoughts become transposed in sensory vividness. What was clearest in the dream seems to me, without further consideration, the most important; but often in some obscure element of the dream I can recognise the most direct offspring of the principal dream thought.

I could only designate this dream displacement as the *transvaluation of psychical values*. The phenomena will not have been considered in all its bearings unless I add that this displacement or transvaluation is shared by different dreams in extremely varying degrees. There are dreams which take place almost without any displacement. These have the same time, meaning, and intelligibility as we found in the dreams which recorded a desire. In other dreams not a bit of the dream idea has retained its own psychical value, or everything essential in these dream ideas has been replaced by unessentials, whilst every kind of transition between these conditions can be found. The more obscure and intricate a dream is, the greater is the part to be ascribed to the impetus of displacement in its formation.

The example that we chose for analysis shows, at least, this much of displacement—that its content has a different centre of interest from that of the dream ideas. In the forefront of the dream content the main scene appears as if a woman wished to make advances to me; in the dream idea the chief interest rests on the desire to enjoy disinterested love which shall "cost nothing"; this idea lies at the back of the talk about the beautiful eyes and the farfetched allusion to "spinach."

If we abolish the dream displacement, we attain through analysis quite certain conclusions regarding two problems of the dream which are most disputed—as to what provokes a dream at all, and as to the connection of the dream with our waking life. There are dreams which at once expose their links with the events of the day; in others no trace of such a connection can be found. By the aid of analysis it can be shown that every dream, without any exception, is linked up with our impression of the day, or perhaps it would be more correct to say of the day previous to the dream. The impressions which have incited the dream may be so important that we are not surprised at our being occupied with them whilst awake; in this case we are right in saying that the dream carries on the chief interest of our waking life. More usually, however, when the dream contains anything relating to the impressions of the day, it is so trivial, unimportant, and so deserving of oblivion, that we can only recall it with an effort. The dream content appears, then, even when coherent and intelligible, to be concerned with those indifferent trifles of thought undeserving of our waking interest. The depreciation of dreams is largely due to the predominance of the indifferent and the worthless in their content.

Analysis destroys the appearance upon which this derogatory judgment is based. When the dream content discloses nothing but some indifferent impression as instigating the dream, analysis ever indicates some significant event, which has been replaced by something indifferent with which it has entered into abundant associations. Where the dream is concerned with uninteresting and unimportant conceptions, analysis reveals the numerous associative paths which connect the trivial with the momentous in the psychical estimation of the individual. *It is only the action of displacement if what is indifferent obtains recognition in the dream content instead of those impressions which are really the stimulus, or instead of the things of real interest.* In answering the question as to what provokes the dream, as to the connection of the dream, in the daily troubles, we must say, in terms of the insight given us by replacing the manifest latent dream content: *The dream does never trouble itself about things which are not deserving of our concern during the day, and trivialities which do not trouble us during the day have no power to pursue us whilst asleep.*

What provoked the dream in the example which we have analysed? The really unimportant event, that a friend invited me to a *free ride in his cab.* The table d'hôte scene in the dream contains an allusion to this indifferent motive, for in conversation I had brought the taxi parallel with the table d'hôte. But I can indicate the important event which has as its substitute the trivial one. A few days before I had disbursed a large sum of money for a member of my family who is very dear to me. Small wonder, says the dream thought, if this person is grateful to me for this—this love is not cost-free. But love that shall cost nothing is one of the prime thoughts of the dream. The fact that shortly before this I had had several *drives* with the relative in question puts the one drive with my friend in a position to recall the connection with the other person. The indifferent impression which, by such ramifications, provokes the dream is subservient to another condition which is not true of the real source of the dream—the impression must be a recent one, everything arising from the day of the dream.

I cannot leave the question of dream displacement without the consideration of a remarkable process in the formation of dreams in which condensation and displacement work together towards one end. In condensation we have already considered the case where two conceptions in the dream having something in common, some point of contact, are replaced in the dream content by a mixed image, where the distinct germ corresponds to what is common, and the indistinct secondary modifications to what is distinctive. If displacement is added to condensation, there is no formation of a mixed image, but a *common mean* which bears the same relationship to the individual elements as does the resultant in the parallelogram of forces to its components. In one of my dreams, for instance, there is talk of an injection with *propyl.*

On first analysis I discovered an indifferent but true incident where *amyl* played a part as the excitant of the dream. I cannot yet vindicate the exchange of amyl for propyl. To the round of ideas of the same dream, however, there belongs the recollection of my first visit to Munich, when the *Propylæa* struck me. The attendant circumstances of the analysis render it admissible that the influence of this second group of conceptions caused the displacement of amyl to propyl. *Propyl* is, so to say, the mean idea between *amyl* and *propylæa*; it got into the dream as a kind of *compromise* by simultaneous condensation and displacement.

The need of discovering some motive for this bewildering work of the dream is even more called for in the case of displacement than in condensation.

VI.

ALTHOUGH THE work of displacement must be held mainly responsible if the dream thoughts are not refound or recognised in the dream content (unless the motive of the changes be guessed), it is another and milder kind of transformation which will be considered with the dream thoughts which leads to the discovery of a new but readily understood act of the dream work. The first dream thoughts which are unravelled by analysis frequently strike one by their unusual wording. They do not appear to be expressed in the sober form which our thinking prefers; rather are they expressed symbolically by allegories and metaphors like the figurative language of the poets. It is not difficult to find the motives for this degree of constraint in the expression of dream ideas. The dream content consists chiefly of visual scenes; hence the dream ideas must, in the first place, be prepared to make use of these forms of presentation. Conceive that a political leader's or a barrister's address had to be transposed into pantomime, and it will be easy to understand the transformations to which the dream work is constrained by regard for this *dramatisation of the dream content*.

Around the psychical stuff of dream thoughts there are ever found reminiscences of impressions, not infrequently of early childhood—scenes which, as a rule, have been visually grasped. Whenever possible, this portion of the dream ideas exercises a definite influence upon the modelling of the dream content; it works like a centre of crystallisation, by attracting and rearranging the stuff of the dream thoughts. The scene of the dream is not infrequently nothing but a modified repetition, complicated by interpolations of events that have left such an impression; the dream but very seldom reproduces accurate and unmixed reproductions of real scenes.

The dream content does not, however, consist exclusively of scenes, but it also includes scattered fragments of visual images, conversations, and even bits of unchanged thoughts. It will be perhaps to the point if we instance in the briefest way the means of dramatisation which are at the disposal of the dream work for the repetition of the dream thoughts in the peculiar language of the dream.

The dream thoughts which we learn from the analysis exhibit themselves as a psychical complex of the most complicated superstructure. Their parts stand in the most diverse relationship to each other; they form backgrounds and foregrounds, stipulations, digressions, illustrations, demonstrations, and protestations. It may be said to be almost the rule that one train of thought is followed by its contradictory. No feature known to our reason whilst awake is absent. If a dream is to grow out of all this, the psychical matter is submitted to a pressure which condenses it extremely, to an inner shrinking and displacement, creating at the same time fresh surfaces, to a selective interweaving among the constituents best adapted for the construction of these scenes. Having regard to the origin of this stuff, the term *regression* can be fairly applied to this process. The logical chains which hitherto held the psychical stuff together become lost in this transformation to the dream content. The dream work takes on, as it were, only the essential content of the dream thoughts for elaboration. It is left to analysis to restore the connection which the dream work has destroyed.

The dream's means of expression must therefore be regarded as meagre in comparison with those of our imagination, though the dream does not renounce all claims to the restitution of logical relation to the dream thoughts. It rather succeeds with tolerable frequency in replacing these by formal characters of its own.

By reason of the undoubted connection existing between all the parts of dream thoughts, the dream is able to embody this matter into a single scene. It upholds a *logical connection as approximation in time and space*, just as the painter, who groups all the poets for his picture of Parnassus who, though they have never been all together on a mountain peak, yet form ideally a community. The dream continues this method of presentation in individual dreams, and often when it displays two elements close together in the dream content it warrants some special inner connection between what they represent in the dream thoughts. It should be, moreover, observed that all the dreams of one night prove on analysis to originate from the same sphere of thought.

The causal connection between two ideas is either left without presentation, or replaced by two different long portions of dreams one after the other. This presentation is frequently a reversed one, the beginning of the dream being the deduction, and its end the hypothesis. The direct *transformation* of one thing into another in the dream seems to serve the relationship of *cause* and *effect*.

The dream never utters the *alternative* "*either-or*," but accepts both as having equal rights in the same connection. When "either-or" is used in the reproduction of dreams, it is, as I have already mentioned, to be replaced by "*and*."

Conceptions which stand in opposition to one another are preferably expressed in dreams by the same element.* There seems no "not" in dreams. Opposition between two ideas, the relation of conversion, is represented in dreams in a very remarkable way. It is expressed by the reversal of another part of the dream content just as if by way of appendix. We shall later on deal with another form of expressing disagreement. The common dream sensation of *movement checked* serves the purpose of representing disagreement of impulses — a *conflict of the will*.

Only one of the logical relationships — that of *similarity, identity, agreement* — is found highly developed in the mechanism of dream formation. Dream work makes use of these cases as a starting-point for condensation, drawing together everything which shows such agreement to a *fresh unity*.

These short, crude observations naturally do not suffice as an estimate of the abundance of the dream's formal means of presenting the logical relationships of the dream thoughts. In this respect, individual dreams are worked up more nicely or more carelessly, our text will have been followed more or less closely, auxiliaries of the dream work will have been taken more or less into consideration. In the latter case they appear obscure, intricate, incoherent. When the dream appears openly absurd, when it contains an obvious paradox in its content, it is so of purpose. Through its apparent disregard of all logical claims, it expresses a part of the intellectual content of the dream ideas. Absurdity in the dream denotes *disagreement, scorn, disdain* in the dream thoughts.

---

*It is worthy of remark that eminent philologists maintain that the oldest languages used the same word for expressing quite general antitheses. In C. Abel's essay, "Ueber den Gegensinn der Urworter" (1884), the following examples of such words in English are given: "gleam—gloom"; "to lock—loch"; "down—The Downs"; "to step—to stop." In his essay on "The Origin of Language" ("Linguistic Essays," p. 240), Abel says: "When the Englishman says 'without,' is not his judgment based upon the comparative juxtaposition of two opposites, 'with' and 'out'; 'with' itself originally meant 'without,' as may still be seen in 'withdraw.' 'Bid' includes the opposite sense of giving and of proffering" (Abel, "The English Verbs of Command," "Linguistic Essays," p. 104; see also Freud, "Ueber den Gegensinn der Urworte": *Jahrbuch für Psychoanalytische und Psychopathologische Forschungen*, Band ii., part i., p. 179). — TRANSLATOR.

As this explanation is in entire disagreement with the view that the dream owes its origin to dissociated, uncritical cerebral activity, I will emphasise my view by an example:

"*One of my acquaintances, Mr. M——, has been attacked by no less a person than Goethe in an essay with, we all maintain, unwarrantable violence. Mr. M—— has naturally been ruined by this attack. He complains very bitterly of this at a dinner-party, but his respect for Goethe has not diminished through this personal experience. I now attempt to clear up the chronological relations which strike me as improbable. Goethe died in 1832. As his attack upon Mr. M—— must, of course, have taken place before, Mr. M—— must have been then a very young man. It seems to me plausible that he was eighteen. I am not certain, however, what year we are actually in, and the whole calculation falls into obscurity. The attack was, moreover, contained in Goethe's well-known essay on 'Nature.'*"

The absurdity of the dream becomes the more glaring when I state that Mr. M—— is a young business man without any poetical or literary interests. My analysis of the dream will show what method there is in this madness. The dream has derived its material from three sources:

1. Mr. M——, to whom I was introduced at a dinner-party, begged me one day to examine his elder brother, who showed signs of mental trouble. In conversation with the patient, an unpleasant episode occurred. Without the slightest occasion he disclosed one of his brother's *youthful escapades*. I had asked the patient the *year of his birth* (*year of death* in dream), and led him to various calculations which might show up his want of memory.

2. A medical journal which displayed my name among others on the cover had published a *ruinous* review of a book by my friend F—— of Berlin, from the pen of a very *juvenile* reviewer. I communicated with the editor, who, indeed, expressed his regret, but would not promise any redress. Thereupon I broke off my connection with the paper; in my letter of resignation I expressed the hope that our *personal relations would not suffer from this*. Here is the real source of the dream. The derogatory reception of my friend's work had made a deep impression upon me. In my judgment, it contained a fundamental biological discovery which only now, several years later, commences to find favour among the professors.

3. A little while before, a patient gave me the medical history of her brother, who, exclaiming "*Nature, Nature!*" had gone out of his mind. The doctors considered that the exclamation arose from a study of Goethe's beautiful essay, and indicated that the patient had been overworking. I expressed the opinion that it seemed more *plausible* to me that the exclamation "Nature!" was to be taken in that sexual meaning

known also to the less educated in our country. It seemed to me that this view had something in it, because the unfortunate youth afterwards mutilated his genital organs. The patient was eighteen years old when the attack occurred.

The first person in the dream thoughts behind the ego was my friend who had been so scandalously treated. "*I now attempted to clear up the chronological relations.*" My friend's book deals with the chronological relations of life, and, amongst other things, correlates *Goethe's* duration of life with a number of days in many ways important to biology. The ego is, however, represented as a general paralytic (*"I am not certain what year we are actually in"*). The dream exhibits my friend as behaving like a general paralytic, and thus riots in absurdity. But the dream thoughts run ironically. "Of course he is a madman, a fool, and you are the genius who understands all about it. But shouldn't it be the *other way round?*" This inversion obviously took place in the dream when Goethe attacked the young man, which is absurd, whilst anyone, however young, can to-day easily attack the great Goethe.

I am prepared to maintain that no dream is inspired by other than egoistic emotions. The ego in the dream does not, indeed, represent only my friend, but stands for myself also. I identify myself with him because the fate of his discovery appears to me typical of the acceptance *of my own.* If I were to publish my own theory, which gives sexuality predominance in the ætiology of psycho-neurotic disorders (see the allusion to the eighteen-year-old patient—"*Nature, Nature!*"), the same criticism would be levelled at me, and it would even now meet with the same contempt.

When I follow out the dream thoughts closely, I ever find only *scorn* and *contempt as correlated with the dream's absurdity.* It is well known that the discovery of a cracked sheep's skull on the Lido in Venice gave Goethe the hint for the so-called vertebral theory of the skull. My friend plumes himself on having as a student raised a hubbub for the resignation of an aged professor who had done good work (including some in this very subject of comparative anatomy), but who, on account of *decrepitude,* had become quite incapable of teaching. The agitation my friend inspired was so successful because in the German Universities an *age limit* is not demanded for academic work. *Age is no protection against folly.* In the hospital here I had for years the honour to serve under a chief who, long fossilised, was for decades notoriously *feeble-minded,* and was yet permitted to continue in his responsible office. A trait, after the manner of the find in the Lido, forces itself upon me here. It was to this man that some youthful colleagues in the hospital adapted the then popular slang of that day: "No Goethe has written that," "No Schiller composed that," etc.

VII.

WE HAVE not exhausted our valuation of the dream work. In addition to condensation, displacement, and definite arrangement of the psychical matter, we must ascribe to it yet another activity—one which is, indeed, not shared by every dream. I shall not treat this position of the dream work exhaustively; I will only point out that the readiest way to arrive at a conception of it is to take for granted, probably unfairly, that it *only subsequently influences the dream content which has already been built up.* Its mode of action thus consists in so co-ordinating the parts of the dream that these coalesce to a coherent whole, to a dream composition. The dream gets a kind of façade which, it is true, does not conceal the whole of its content. There is a sort of preliminary explanation to be strengthened by interpolations and slight alterations. Such elaboration of the dream content must not be too pronounced; the misconception of the dream thoughts to which it gives rise is merely superficial, and our first piece of work in analysing a dream is to get rid of these early attempts at interpretation.

The motives for this part of the dream work are easily gauged. This final elaboration of the dream is due to a *regard for intelligibility*—a fact at once betraying the origin of an action which behaves towards the actual dream content just as our normal psychical action behaves towards some proferred perception that is to our liking. The dream content is thus secured under the pretence of certain expectations, is perceptually classified by the supposition of its intelligibility, thereby risking its falsification, whilst, in fact, the most extraordinary misconceptions arise if the dream can be correlated with nothing familiar. Everyone is aware that we are unable to look at any series of unfamiliar signs, or to listen to a discussion of unknown words, without at once making perpetual changes through *our regard for intelligibility*, through our falling back upon what is familiar.

We can call those dreams *properly made up* which are the result of an elaboration in every way analogous to the psychical action of our waking life. In other dreams there is no such action; not even an attempt is made to bring about order and meaning. We regard the dream as "quite mad," because on awaking it is with this last-named part of the dream work, the dream elaboration, that we identify ourselves. So far, however, as our analysis is concerned, the dream, which resembles a medley of disconnected fragments, is of as much value as the one with a smooth and beautifully polished surface. In the former case we are spared, to some extent, the trouble of breaking down the super-elaboration of the dream content.

All the same, it would be an error to see in the dream façade nothing but the misunderstood and somewhat arbitrary elaboration of the dream carried out at the instance of our psychical life. Wishes and phantasies are not infrequently employed in the erection of this façade, which were already fashioned in the dream thoughts; they are akin to those of our waking life—"day-dreams," as they are very properly called. These wishes and phantasies, which analysis discloses in our dreams at night, often present themselves as repetitions and refashionings of the scenes of infancy. Thus the dream façade may show us directly the true core of the dream, distorted through admixture with other matter.

Beyond these four activities there is nothing else to be discovered in the dream work. If we keep closely to the definition that dream work denotes the transference of dream thoughts to dream content, we are compelled to say that the dream work is not creative; it develops no fancies of its own, it judges nothing, decides nothing. It does nothing but prepare the matter for condensation and displacement, and refashions it for dramatisation, to which must be added the inconstant last-named mechanism—that of explanatory elaboration. It is true that a good deal is found in the dream content which might be understood as the result of another and more intellectual performance; but analysis shows conclusively every time that these *intellectual operations were already present in the dream thoughts, and have only been taken over by the dream content*. A syllogism in the dream is nothing other than the repetition of a syllogism in the dream thoughts; it seems inoffensive if it has been transferred to the dream without alteration; it becomes absurd if in the dream work it has been transferred to other matter. A calculation in the dream content simply means that there was a calculation in the dream thoughts; whilst this is always correct, the calculation in the dream can furnish the silliest results by the condensation of its factors and the displacement of the same operations to other things. Even speeches which are found in the dream content are not new compositions; they prove to be pieced together out of speeches which have been made or heard or read; the words are faithfully copied, but the occasion of their utterance is quite overlooked, and their meaning is most violently changed.

It is, perhaps, not superfluous to support these assertions by examples:

1. *A seemingly inoffensive, well-made dream of a patient. She was going to market with her cook, who carried the basket. The butcher said to her when she asked him for something: "That is all gone," and wished to give her something else, remarking: "That's very good." She declines, and goes to the greengrocer, who wants to sell her a peculiar vegetable which is bound up in bundles and of a black colour. She says: "I don't know that; I won't take it."*

The remark "That is all gone" arose from the treatment. A few days before I said myself to the patient that the earliest reminiscences of childhood *are all gone* as such, but are replaced by transferences and dreams. Thus I am the butcher.

The second remark, "*I don't know that,*" arose in a very different connection. The day before she had herself called out in rebuke to the cook (who, moreover, also appears in the dream): "*Behave yourself properly;* I don't know *that*"—that is, "I don't know this kind of behaviour; I won't have it." The more harmless portion of this speech was arrived at by a displacement of the dream content; in the dream thoughts only the other portion of the speech played a part, because the dream work changed an imaginary situation into utter irrecognisability and complete inoffensiveness (while in a certain sense I behave in an unseemly way to the lady). The situation resulting in this phantasy is, however, nothing but a new edition of one that actually took place.

2. *A dream apparently meaningless relates to figures. "She wants to pay something; her daughter takes three florins sixty-five kreuzers out of her purse; but she says: 'What are you doing? It only costs twenty-one kreuzers.'"*

The dreamer was a stranger who had placed her child at school in Vienna, and who was able to continue under my treatment so long as her daughter remained at Vienna. The day before the dream the directress of the school had recommended her to keep the child another year at school. In this case she would have been able to prolong her treatment by one year. The figures in the dream become important if it be remembered that time is money. One year equals 365 days, or, expressed in kreuzers, 365 kreuzers, which is three florins sixty-five kreuzers. The twenty-one kreuzers correspond with the three weeks which remained from the day of the dream to the end of the school term, and thus to the end of the treatment. It was obviously financial considerations which had moved the lady to refuse the proposal of the directress, and which were answerable for the triviality of the amount in the dream.

3. A lady, young, but already ten years married, heard that a friend of hers, Miss Elise L——, of about the same age, had become engaged. This gave rise to the following dream:

She was sitting with her husband in the theatre; the one side of the stalls was quite empty. Her husband tells her, Elise L—— and her fiancé had intended coming, but could only get some cheap seats, three for one florin fifty kreuzers, and these they would not take. In her opinion, that would not have mattered very much.

The origin of the figures from the matter of the dream thoughts and the changes the figures underwent are of interest. Whence came the one florin fifty kreuzers? From a trifling occurrence of the previous day. Her sister-in-law had received 150 florins as a present from her husband, and had quickly got rid of it by buying some ornament. Note that 150 florins is one hundred times one florin fifty kreuzers. For the *three* concerned with the tickets, the only link is that Elise L—— is exactly three months younger than the dreamer. The scene in the dream is the repetition of a little adventure for which she has often been teased by her husband. She was once in a great hurry to get tickets in time for a piece, and when she came to the theatre *one side of the stalls was almost empty*. It was therefore quite unnecessary for her to have been in *such a hurry*. Nor must we overlook the absurdity of the dream that two persons should take three tickets for the theatre.

Now for the dream ideas. It was *stupid* to have married so early; I *need not* have been *in so great a hurry*. Elise L——'s example shows me that I should have been able to get a husband later; indeed, one a *hundred times better* if I had but waited. I could have bought *three* such men with the money (dowry).

VIII.

IN THE foregoing exposition we have now learnt something of the dream work; we must regard it as a quite special psychical process, which, so far as we are aware, resembles nothing else. To the dream work has been transferred that bewilderment which its product, the dream, has aroused in us. In truth, the dream work is only the first recognition of a group of psychical processes to which must be referred the origin of hysterical symptoms, the ideas of morbid dread, obsession, and illusion. Condensation, and especially displacement, are never-failing features in these other processes. The regard for appearance remains, on the other hand, peculiar to the dream work. If this explanation brings the dream into line with the formation of psychical disease, it becomes the more important to fathom the essential conditions of processes like dream building. It will be probably a surprise to hear that neither the state of sleep nor illness is among the indispensable conditions. A whole number of phenomena of the everyday life of healthy persons, forgetfulness, slips in speaking and in holding things, together with a certain class of mistakes, are due to a psychical mechanism analogous to that of the dream and the other members of this group.

Displacement is the core of the problem, and the most striking of all the dream performances. A thorough investigation of the subject shows that the essential condition of displacement is purely psychological; it is in the nature of a motive. We get on the track by thrashing out experiences which one cannot avoid in the analysis of dreams. I had to break off the relations of my dream thoughts in the analysis of my dream on p. 5 because I found some experiences which I do not wish strangers to know, and which I could not relate without serious damage to important considerations. I added, it would be no use were I to select another instead of that particular dream; in every dream where the content is obscure or intricate, I should hit upon dream thoughts which call for secrecy. If, however, I continue the analysis for myself, without regard to those others, for whom, indeed, so personal an event as my dream cannot matter, I arrive finally at ideas which surprise me, which I have not known to be mine, which not only appear *foreign* to me, but which are *unpleasant,* and which I would like to oppose vehemently, whilst the chain of ideas running through the analysis intrudes upon me inexorably. I can only take these circumstances into account by admitting that these thoughts are actually part of my psychical life, possessing a certain psychical intensity or energy. However, by virtue of a particular psychological condition, the *thoughts could not become conscious to me.* I call this particular condition "Repression." It is therefore impossible for me not to recognise some causal relationship between the obscurity of the dream content and this state of repression—this *incapacity of consciousness.* When I conclude that the cause of the obscurity is *the desire to conceal these thoughts.* Thus I arrive at the conception of the *dream distortion* as the deed of the dream work, and of *displacement* serving to disguise this object.

I will test this in my own dream, and ask myself, What is the thought which, quite innocuous in its distorted form, provokes my liveliest opposition in its real form? I remember that the free drive reminded me of the last expensive drive with a member of my family, the interpretation of the dream being: I should for once like to experience affection for which I should not have to pay, and that shortly before the dream I had to make a heavy disbursement for this very person. In this connection, I cannot get away from the thought *that I regret this disbursement.* It is only when I acknowledge this feeling that there is any sense in my wishing in the dream for an affection that should entail no outlay. And yet I can state on my honour that I did not hesitate for a moment when it became necessary to expend that sum. The regret, the counter-current, was unconscious to me. Why it was unconscious is quite another question which would lead us far away from the answer which, though within my knowledge, belongs elsewhere.

If I subject the dream of another person instead of one of my own to analysis, the result is the same; the motives for convincing others is, however, changed. In the dream of a healthy person the only way for me to enable him to accept this repressed idea is the coherence of the dream thoughts. He is at liberty to reject this explanation. But if we are dealing with a person suffering from any neurosis—say from hysteria— the recognition of these repressed ideas is compulsory by reason of their connection with the symptoms of his illness and of the improvement resulting from exchanging the symptoms for the repressed ideas. Take the patient from whom I got the last dream about the three tickets for one florin fifty kreuzers. Analysis shows that she does not think highly of her husband, that she regrets having married him, that she would be glad to change him for someone else. It is true that she maintains that she loves her husband, that her emotional life knows nothing about this depreciation (a hundred times better!), but all her symptoms lead to the same conclusion as this dream. When her repressed memories had rewakened a certain period when she was conscious that she did not love her husband, her symptoms disappeared, and therewith disappeared her resistance to the interpretation of the dream.

IX.

THIS CONCEPTION of repression once fixed, together with the distortion of the dream in relation to repressed psychical matter, we are in a position to give a general exposition of the principal results which the analysis of dreams supplies. We learnt that the most intelligible and meaningful dreams are unrealised desires; the desires they pictured as realised are known to consciousness, have been held over from the daytime, and are of absorbing interest. The analysis of obscure and intricate dreams discloses something very similar; the dream scene again pictures as realised some desire which regularly proceeds from the dream ideas, but the picture is unrecognisable, and is only cleared up in the analysis. The desire itself is either one repressed, foreign to consciousness, or it is closely bound up with repressed ideas. The formula for these dreams may be thus stated: *They are concealed realisations of repressed desires.* It is interesting to note that they are right who regard the dream as foretelling the future. Although the future which the dream shows us is not that which will occur, but that which we would like to occur. Folk psychology proceeds here according to its wont; it believes what it wishes to believe.

Dreams can be divided into three classes according to their relation towards the realisation of desire. Firstly come those which exhibit a *non-repressed, non-concealed desire*; these are dreams of the infantile type, becoming ever rarer among adults. Secondly, dreams which express in *veiled* form some *repressed desire*; these constitute by far the larger number of our dreams, and they require analysis for their understanding. Thirdly, these dreams where repression exists, but *without* or with but slight concealment. These dreams are invariably accompanied by a feeling of dread which brings the dream to an end. This feeling of dread here replaces dream displacement; I regarded the dream

34

work as having prevented this in the dream of the second class. It is not very difficult to prove that what is now present as intense dread in the dream was once desire, and is now secondary to the repression.

There are also definite dreams with a painful content, without the presence of any anxiety in the dream. These cannot be reckoned among dreams of dread; they have, however, always been used to prove the unimportance and the psychical futility of dreams. An analysis of such an example will show that it belongs to our second class of dreams—a *perfectly concealed* realisation of repressed desires. Analysis will demonstrate at the same time how excellently adapted is the work of displacement to the concealment of desires.

A girl dreamt that she saw lying dead before her the only surviving child of her sister amid the same surroundings as a few years before she saw the first child lying dead. She was not sensible of any pain, but naturally combated the view that the scene represented a desire of hers. Nor was that view necessary. Years ago it was at the funeral of the child that she had last seen and spoken to the man she loved. Were the second child to die, she would be sure to meet this man again in her sister's house. She is longing to meet him, but struggles against this feeling. The day of the dream she had taken a ticket for a lecture, which announced the presence of the man she always loved. The dream is simply a dream of impatience common to those which happen before a journey, theatre, or simply anticipated pleasures. The longing is concealed by the shifting of the scene to the occasion when any joyous feeling were out of place, and yet where it did once exist. Note, further, that the emotional behaviour in the dream is adapted, not to the displaced, but to the real but suppressed dream ideas. The scene anticipates the long-hoped-for meeting; there is here no call for painful emotions.

X.

THERE HAS hitherto been no occasion for philosophers to bestir themselves with a psychology of repression. We must be allowed to construct some clear conception as to the origin of dreams as the first steps in this unknown territory. The scheme which we have formulated not only from a study of dreams is, it is true, already somewhat complicated, but we cannot find any simpler one that will suffice. We hold that our psychical apparatus contains two procedures for the construction of thoughts. The second one has the advantage that its products find an open path to consciousness, whilst the activity of the first procedure is unknown to itself, and can only arrive at consciousness through the second one. At the borderland of these two procedures, where the first passes over into the second, a censorship is established which only passes what pleases it, keeping back everything else. That which is rejected by the censorship is, according to our definition, in a state of repression. Under certain conditions, one of which is the sleeping state, the balance of power between the two procedures is so changed that what is repressed can no longer be kept back. In the sleeping state this may possibly occur through the negligence of the censor; what has been hitherto repressed will now succeed in finding its way to consciousness. But as the censorship is never absent, but merely off guard, certain alterations must be conceded so as to placate it. It is a compromise which becomes conscious in this case—a compromise between what one procedure has in view and the demands of the other. *Repression, laxity of the censor, compromise*—this is the foundation for the origin of many another psychological process, just as it is for the dream. In such compromises we can observe the processes of condensation, of displacement, the acceptance of superficial associations, which we have found in the dream work.

36

It is not for us to deny the demonic element which has played a part in constructing our explanation of dream work. The impression left is that the formation of obscure dreams proceeds as if a person had something to say which must be disagreeable for another person upon whom he is dependent to hear. It is by the use of this image that we figure to ourselves the conception of the *dream distortion* and of the censorship, and ventured to crystallise our impression in a rather crude, but at least definite, psychological theory. Whatever explanation the future may offer of these first and second procedures, we shall expect a confirmation of our correlate that the second procedure commands the entrance to consciousness, and can exclude the first from consciousness.

Once the sleeping state overcome, the censorship resumes complete sway, and is now able to revoke that which was granted in a moment of weakness. That the *forgetting* of dreams explains this in part, at least, we are convinced by our experience, confirmed again and again. During the relation of a dream, or during analysis of one, it not infrequently happens that some fragment of the dream is suddenly forgotten. This fragment so forgotten invariably contains the best and readiest approach to an understanding of the dream. Probably that is why it sinks into oblivion—*i.e.*, into a renewed suppression.

XI.

VIEWING THE dream content as the representation of a realised desire, and referring its vagueness to the changes made by the censor in the repressed matter, it is no longer difficult to grasp the function of dreams. In fundamental contrast with those saws which assume that sleep is disturbed by dreams, we hold the *dream as the guardian of sleep*. So far as children's dreams are concerned, our view should find ready acceptance.

The sleeping state or the psychical change to sleep, whatsoever it be, is brought about by the child being sent to sleep or compelled thereto by fatigue, only assisted by the removal of all stimuli which might open other objects to the psychical apparatus. The means which serve to keep external stimuli distant are known; but what are the means we can employ to depress the internal psychical stimuli which frustrate sleep? Look at a mother getting her child to sleep. The child is full of beseeching; he wants another kiss; he wants to play yet awhile. His requirements are in part met, in part drastically put off till the following day. Clearly these desires and needs, which agitate him, are hindrances to sleep. Everyone knows the charming story of the bad boy (Baldwin Groller's) who awoke at night bellowing out, "*I want the rhinoceros*." A really good boy, instead of bellowing, would have *dreamt* that he was playing with the rhinoceros. Because the dream which realises his desire is believed during sleep, it removes the desire and makes sleep possible. It cannot be denied that this belief accords with the dream image, because it is arrayed in the psychical appearance of probability; the child is without the capacity which it will acquire later to distinguish hallucinations or phantasies from reality.

The adult has learnt this differentiation; he has also learnt the futility of desire, and by continuous practice manages to postpone his aspirations, until they can be granted in some roundabout method by a change in the external world. For this reason it is rare for him to have his wishes realised during sleep in the short psychical way. It is even possible that this never happens, and that everything which appears to us like a child's dream demands a much more elaborate explanation. Thus it is that for adults—for every sane person without exception—a differentiation of the psychical matter has been fashioned which the child knew not. A psychical procedure has been reached which, informed by the experience of life, exercises with jealous power a dominating and restraining influence upon psychical emotions; by its relation to consciousness, and by its spontaneous mobility, it is endowed with the greatest means of psychical power. A portion of the infantile emotions has been withheld from this procedure as useless to life, and all the thoughts which flow from these are found in the state of repression.

Whilst the procedure in which we recognise our normal ego reposes upon the desire for sleep, it appears compelled by the psycho-physiological conditions of sleep to abandon some of the energy with which it was wont during the day to keep down what was repressed. This neglect is really harmless; however much the emotions of the child's spirit may be stirred, they find the approach to consciousness rendered difficult, and that to movement blocked in consequence of the state of sleep. The danger of their disturbing sleep must, however, be avoided. Moreover, we must admit that even in deep sleep some amount of free attention is exerted as a protection against sense-stimuli which might, perchance, make an awakening seem wiser than the continuance of sleep. Otherwise we could not explain the fact of our being always awakened by stimuli of certain quality. As the old physiologist Burdach pointed out, the mother is awakened by the whimpering of her child, the miller by the cessation of his mill, most people by gently calling out their names. This attention, thus on the alert, makes use of the internal stimuli arising from repressed desires, and fuses them into the dream, which as a compromise satisfies both procedures at the same time. The dream creates a form of psychical release for the wish which is either suppressed or formed by the aid of repression, inasmuch as it presents it as realised. The other procedure is also satisfied, since the continuance of the sleep is assured. Our ego here gladly behaves like a child; it makes the dream pictures believable, saying, as it were, "Quite right, but let me sleep." The contempt which, once awakened, we bear the dream, and which rests upon the absurdity and apparent illogicality of the dream, is probably nothing but the reasoning of our sleeping ego on the feelings about what was repressed; with greater right it should rest upon the incompetency of this disturber of our sleep. In sleep we are now and then aware of this contempt; the dream content transcends the censorship rather too much, we think, "It's only a dream," and sleep on.

It is no objection to this view if there are border-lines for the dream where its function, to preserve sleep from interruption, can no longer be maintained—as in the dreams of impending dread. It is here changed for another function—to suspend the sleep at the proper time. It acts like a conscientious night-watchman, who first does his duty by quelling disturbances so as not to waken the citizen, but equally does his duty quite properly when he awakens the street should the causes of the trouble seem to him serious and himself unable to cope with them alone.

This function of dreams becomes especially well marked when there arises some incentive for the sense perception. That the senses aroused during sleep influence the dream is well known, and can be experimentally verified; it is one of the certain but much overestimated results of the medical investigation of dreams. Hitherto there has been an insoluble riddle connected with this discovery. The stimulus to the sense by which the investigator affects the sleeper is not properly recognised in the dream, but is intermingled with a number of indefinite interpretations, whose determination appears left to psychical free-will. There is, of course, no such psychical free-will. To an external sense-stimulus the sleeper can react in many ways. Either he awakens or he succeeds in sleeping on. In the latter case he can make use of the dream to dismiss the external stimulus, and this, again, in more ways than one. For instance, he can stay the stimulus by dreaming of a scene which is absolutely intolerable to him. This was the means used by one who was troubled by a painful perineal abscess. He dreamt that he was on horseback, and made use of the poultice, which was intended to alleviate his pain, as a saddle, and thus got away from the cause of the trouble. Or, as is more frequently the case, the external stimulus undergoes a new rendering, which leads him to connect it with a repressed desire seeking its realisation, and robs him of its reality, and is treated as if it were a part of the psychical matter. Thus, someone dreamt that he had written a comedy which embodied a definite *motif*; it was being performed; the first act was over amid enthusiastic applause; there was great clapping. At this moment the dreamer must have succeeded in prolonging his sleep despite the disturbance, for when he woke he no longer heard the noise; he concluded rightly that someone must have been beating a carpet or bed. The dreams which come with a loud noise just before waking have all attempted to cover the stimulus to waking by some other explanation, and thus to prolong the sleep for a little while.

XII.

WHOSOEVER HAS firmly accepted this *censorship* as the chief motive for the distortion of dreams will not be surprised to learn as the result of dream interpretation that most of the dreams of adults are traced by analysis to erotic desires. This assertion is not drawn from dreams obviously of a sexual nature, which are known to all dreamers from their own experience, and are the only ones usually described as "sexual dreams." These dreams are ever sufficiently mysterious by reason of the choice of persons who are made the objects of sex, the removal of all the barriers which cry halt to the dreamer's sexual needs in his waking state, the many strange reminders as to details of what are called perversions. But analysis discovers that, in many other dreams in whose manifest content nothing erotic can be found, the work of interpretation shows them up as, in reality, realisation of sexual desires; whilst, on the other hand, that much of the thought-making when awake, the thoughts saved us as surplus from the day only, reaches presentation in dreams with the help of repressed erotic desires.

Towards the explanation of this statement, which is no theoretical postulate, it must be remembered that no other class of instincts has required so vast a suppression at the behest of civilisation as the sexual, whilst their mastery by the highest psychical processes are in most persons soonest of all relinquished. Since we have learnt to understand *infantile sexuality*, often so vague in its expression, so invariably overlooked and misunderstood, we are justified in saying that nearly every civilised person has retained at some point or other the infantile type of sex life; thus we understand that repressed infantile sex desires furnish the most frequent and most powerful impulses for the formation of dreams.*

---

*Freud, "Three Contributions to Sexual Theory," translated by A. A. Brill (*Journal of Nervous and Mental Disease* Publishing Company, New York).

If the dream, which is the expression of some erotic desire, succeeds in making its manifest content appear innocently asexual, it is only possible in one way. The matter of these sexual presentations cannot be exhibited as such, but must be replaced by allusions, suggestions, and similar indirect means; differing from other cases of indirect presentation, those used in dreams must be deprived of direct understanding. The means of presentation which answer these requirements are commonly termed "symbols." A special interest has been directed towards these, since it has been observed that the dreamers of the same language use the like symbols—indeed, that in certain cases community of symbol is greater than community of speech. Since the dreamers do not themselves know the meaning of the symbols they use, it remains a puzzle whence arises their relationship with what they replace and denote. The fact itself is undoubted, and becomes of importance for the technique of the interpretation of dreams, since by the aid of a knowledge of this symbolism it is possible to understand the meaning of the elements of a dream, or parts of a dream, occasionally even the whole dream itself, without having to question the dreamer as to his own ideas. We thus come near to the popular idea of an interpretation of dreams, and, on the other hand, possess again the technique of the ancients, among whom the interpretation of dreams was identical with their explanation through symbolism.

Though the study of dream symbolism is far removed from finality, we now possess a series of general statements and of particular observations which are quite certain. There are symbols which practically always have the same meaning: Emperor and Empress (King and Queen) always mean the parents; room, a woman,* and so on. The sexes are represented by a great variety of symbols, many of which would be at first quite incomprehensible had not the clues to the meaning been often obtained through other channels.

There are symbols of universal circulation, found in all dreamers, of one range of speech and culture; there are others of the narrowest individual significance which an individual has built up out of his own material. In the first class those can be differentiated whose claim can be at once recognised by the replacement of sexual things in common speech (those, for instance, arising from agriculture, as reproduction, seed) from others whose sexual references appear to reach back to the

---

*The words from "and" to "channels" in the next sentence is a short summary of the passage in the original. As this book will be read by other than professional people the passage has not been translated, in deference to English opinion.—TRANSLATOR.

earliest times and to the obscurest depths of our image-building. The power of building symbols in both these special forms of symbols has not died out. Recently discovered things, like the airship, are at once brought into universal use as sex symbols.

It would be quite an error to suppose that a profounder knowledge of dream symbolism (the "Language of Dreams") would make us independent of questioning the dreamer regarding his impressions about the dream, and would give us back the whole technique of ancient dream interpreters. Apart from individual symbols and the variations in the use of what is general, one never knows whether an element in the dream is to be understood symbolically or in its proper meaning; the whole content of the dream is certainly not to be interpreted symbolically. The knowledge of dream symbols will only help us in understanding portions of the dream content, and does not render the use of the technical rules previously given at all superfluous. But it must be of the greatest service in interpreting a dream just when the impressions of the dreamer are withheld or are insufficient.

Dream symbolism proves also indispensable for understanding the so-called "typical" dreams and the dreams that "repeat themselves." If the value of the symbolism of dreams has been so incompletely set out in this belief portrayal, this attempt will be corrected by reference to a point of view which is of the highest import in this connection. Dream symbolism leads us far beyond the dream; it does not belong only to dreams, but is likewise dominant in legend, myth, and saga, in wit and in folklore. It compels us to pursue the inner meaning of the dream in these productions. But we must acknowledge that symbolism is not a result of the dream work, but is a peculiarity probably of our unconscious thinking, which furnishes to the dream work the matter for condensation, displacement, and dramatisation.

XIII.

I DISCLAIM all pretension to have thrown light here upon all the problems of the dream, or to have dealt convincingly with everything here touched upon. If anyone is interested in the whole of dream literature, I refer him to the works of Sante de Sanctis (I sogni, Turin, 1899). For a more complete investigation of my conception of the dream, my work should be consulted: "Die Traumdeutung," Leipzig and Vienna, third edition, 1911.* I will only point out in what direction my exposition on dream work should be followed up.

If I posit as the problem of dream interpretation the replacement of the dream by its latent ideas—that is, the resolution of that which the dream work has woven—I raise a series of new psychological problems which refer to the mechanism of this dream work as well as to the nature and the conditions of this so-called repression. On the other hand, I claim the existence of dream thoughts as a very valuable foundation for psychical construction of the highest order, provided with all the signs of normal intellectual performance. This matter is, however, removed from consciousness until it is rendered in the distorted form of the dream content. I am compelled to believe that all persons have such ideas, since nearly all, even the most normal, can have dreams. To the unconsciousness of dream ideas, or their relationship to consciousness and to repression, are linked questions of the greatest psychological importance. Their solution must be postponed until the analysis of the origin of other psychopathic growths, such as the symptoms of hysteria and of obsessions, has been made clear.

---

*Freud, "The Interpretation of Dreams," third edition, translated by A. A. Brill. London: George Allen and Company, Ltd.

Literature

For a completer study of Dream Symbolism, consult the work of Artemidorus Daldianus: The Interpretation of Dreams. Rendered into English by "R. W."—*i.e.*, Robert Wood. The fourth edition, newly written. B. L., London, 1644. The last edition was published in 1786.

SCHERNER, R. A. Das Leben des Traumes. Berlin, 1861.

FREUD. The Interpretation of Dreams.

For the symbolism of legend, myth, and saga compared with dreams, see—

ABRAHAM, KARL. Traum und Mythus.

RANK, OTTO. Der Mythus von der Geburt des Helden.

RIKLIN, F. Wunscherfüllung und Symbolik im Märchen.

These three works are published by Franz Deuticke, Vienna. English translations are ready, or are in preparation.

Recent literature will be found in—

Jahrbuch für Psychoanalytische und Psychopathologische Forschungen: Franz Deuticke.
Internationale Zeitschrift für Ärztliche Psychoanalyse; and Imago (both published by Hugo Heller and Co., Vienna).

DOVER · THRIFT · EDITIONS

POETRY

A Shropshire Lad, A. E. Housman. 64pp. 26468-8 $1.00

Lyric Poems, John Keats. 80pp. 26871-3 $1.00

Gunga Din and Other Favorite Poems, Rudyard Kipling. 80pp. 26471-8 $1.00

The Congo and Other Poems, Vachel Lindsay. 96pp. 27272-9 $1.50

Evangeline and Other Poems, Henry Wadsworth Longfellow. 64pp. 28255-4 $1.00

Favorite Poems, Henry Wadsworth Longfellow. 96pp. 27273-7 $1.00

"To His Coy Mistress" and Other Poems, Andrew Marvell. 64pp. 29544-3 $1.00

Spoon River Anthology, Edgar Lee Masters. 144pp. 27275-3 $1.50

Renascence and Other Poems, Edna St. Vincent Millay. 64pp. (Available in U.S. only.) 26873-X $1.00

Selected Poems, John Milton. 128pp. 27554-X $1.50

Civil War Poetry: An Anthology, Paul Negri (ed.). 128pp. 29883-3 $1.50

English Victorian Poetry: An Anthology, Paul Negri (ed.). 256pp. 40425-0 $2.00

Great Sonnets, Paul Negri (ed.). 96pp. 28052-7 $1.00

The Raven and Other Favorite Poems, Edgar Allan Poe. 64pp. 26685-0 $1.00

Essay on Man and Other Poems, Alexander Pope. 128pp. 28053-5 $1.50

Early Poems, Ezra Pound. 80pp. (Available in U.S. only.) 28745-9 $1.00

Great Poems by American Women: An Anthology, Susan L. Rattiner (ed.). 224pp. (Available in U.S. only.) 40164-2 $2.00

Little Orphant Annie and Other Poems, James Whitcomb Riley. 80pp. 28260-0 $1.00

"Miniver Cheevy" and Other Poems, Edwin Arlington Robinson. 64pp. 28756-4 $1.00

Goblin Market and Other Poems, Christina Rossetti. 64pp. 28055-1 $1.00

Chicago Poems, Carl Sandburg. 80pp. 28057-8 $1.00

The Shooting of Dan McGrew and Other Poems, Robert Service. 96pp. (Available in U.S. only.) 27556-6 $1.50

Complete Sonnets, William Shakespeare. 80pp. 26686-9 $1.00

Selected Poems, Percy Bysshe Shelley. 128pp. 27558-2 $1.50

African-American Poetry: An Anthology, 1773–1930, Joan R. Sherman (ed.). 96pp. 29604-0 $1.00

100 Best-Loved Poems, Philip Smith (ed.). 96pp. 28553-7 $1.00

Native American Songs and Poems: An Anthology, Brian Swann (ed.). 64pp. 29450-1 $1.00

Selected Poems, Alfred Lord Tennyson. 112pp. 27282-6 $1.50

Aeneid, Vergil (Publius Vergilius Maro). 256pp. 28749-1 $2.00

Christmas Carols: Complete Verses, Shane Weller (ed.). 64pp. 27397-0 $1.00

Great Love Poems, Shane Weller (ed.). 128pp. 27284-2 $1.00

Civil War Poetry and Prose, Walt Whitman. 96pp. 28507-3 $1.00

Selected Poems, Walt Whitman. 128pp. 26878-0 $1.00

The Ballad of Reading Gaol and Other Poems, Oscar Wilde. 64pp. 27072-6 $1.00

Early Poems, William Carlos Williams. 64pp. (Available in U.S. only.) 29294-0 $1.00

Favorite Poems, William Wordsworth. 80pp. 27073-4 $1.00

World War One British Poets: Brooke, Owen, Sassoon, Rosenberg, and Others, Candace Ward (ed.). (Available in U.S. only.) 29568-0 $1.00

Early Poems, William Butler Yeats. 128pp. 27808-5 $1.50

"Easter, 1916" and Other Poems, William Butler Yeats. 80pp. (Available in U.S. only.) 29771-3 $1.00

DOVER · THRIFT · EDITIONS

FICTION

FLATLAND: A ROMANCE OF MANY DIMENSIONS, Edwin A. Abbott. 96pp. 27263-X $1.00

SHORT STORIES, Louisa May Alcott. 64pp. 29063-8 $1.00

WINESBURG, OHIO, Sherwood Anderson. 160pp. 28269-4 $2.00

PERSUASION, Jane Austen. 224pp. 29555-9 $2.00

PRIDE AND PREJUDICE, Jane Austen. 272pp. 28473-5 $2.00

SENSE AND SENSIBILITY, Jane Austen. 272pp. 29049-2 $2.00

LOOKING BACKWARD, Edward Bellamy. 160pp. 29038-7 $2.00

BEOWULF, Beowulf (trans. by R. K. Gordon). 64pp. 27264-8 $1.00

CIVIL WAR STORIES, Ambrose Bierce. 128pp. 28038-1 $1.00

"THE MOONLIT ROAD" AND OTHER GHOST AND HORROR STORIES, Ambrose Bierce (John Grafton, ed.) 96pp. 40056-5 $1.00

WUTHERING HEIGHTS, Emily Brontë. 256pp. 29256-8 $2.00

THE THIRTY-NINE STEPS, John Buchan. 96pp. 28201-5 $1.50

TARZAN OF THE APES, Edgar Rice Burroughs. 224pp. (Available in U.S. only.) 29570-2 $2.00

ALICE'S ADVENTURES IN WONDERLAND, Lewis Carroll. 96pp. 27543-4 $1.00

THROUGH THE LOOKING-GLASS, Lewis Carroll. 128pp. 40878-7 $1.50

MY ÁNTONIA, Willa Cather. 176pp. 28240-6 $2.00

O PIONEERS!, Willa Cather. 128pp. 27785-2 $1.00

PAUL'S CASE AND OTHER STORIES, Willa Cather. 64pp. 29057-3 $1.00

FIVE GREAT SHORT STORIES, Anton Chekhov. 96pp. 26463-7 $1.00

TALES OF CONJURE AND THE COLOR LINE, Charles Waddell Chesnutt. 128pp. 40426-9 $1.50

FAVORITE FATHER BROWN STORIES, G. K. Chesterton. 96pp. 27545-0 $1.00

THE AWAKENING, Kate Chopin. 128pp. 27786-0 $1.00

A PAIR OF SILK STOCKINGS AND OTHER STORIES, Kate Chopin. 64pp. 29264-9 $1.00

HEART OF DARKNESS, Joseph Conrad. 80pp. 26464-5 $1.00

LORD JIM, Joseph Conrad. 256pp. 40650-4 $2.00

THE SECRET SHARER AND OTHER STORIES, Joseph Conrad. 128pp. 27546-9 $1.00

THE "LITTLE REGIMENT" AND OTHER CIVIL WAR STORIES, Stephen Crane. 80pp. 29557-5 $1.00

THE OPEN BOAT AND OTHER STORIES, Stephen Crane. 128pp. 27547-7 $1.50

THE RED BADGE OF COURAGE, Stephen Crane. 112pp. 26465-3 $1.00

MOLL FLANDERS, Daniel Defoe. 256pp. 29093-X $2.00

ROBINSON CRUSOE, Daniel Defoe. 288pp. 40427-7 $2.00

A CHRISTMAS CAROL, Charles Dickens. 80pp. 26865-9 $1.00

THE CRICKET ON THE HEARTH AND OTHER CHRISTMAS STORIES, Charles Dickens. 128pp. 28039-X $1.00

A TALE OF TWO CITIES, Charles Dickens. 304pp. 40651-2 $2.00

THE DOUBLE, Fyodor Dostoyevsky. 128pp. 29572-9 $1.50

THE GAMBLER, Fyodor Dostoyevsky. 112pp. 29081-6 $1.50

NOTES FROM THE UNDERGROUND, Fyodor Dostoyevsky. 96pp. 27053-X $1.00

THE ADVENTURE OF THE DANCING MEN AND OTHER STORIES, Sir Arthur Conan Doyle. 80pp. 29558-3 $1.00

THE HOUND OF THE BASKERVILLES, Arthur Conan Doyle. 128pp. 28214-7 $1.50

THE LOST WORLD, Arthur Conan Doyle. 176pp. 40060-3 $1.50

DOVER · THRIFT · EDITIONS

FICTION

SIX GREAT SHERLOCK HOLMES STORIES, Sir Arthur Conan Doyle. 112pp. 27055-6 $1.00

SILAS MARNER, George Eliot. 160pp. 29246-0 $1.50

THIS SIDE OF PARADISE, F. Scott Fitzgerald. 208pp. 28999-0 $2.00

"THE DIAMOND AS BIG AS THE RITZ" AND OTHER STORIES, F. Scott Fitzgerald. 29991-0 $2.00

THE REVOLT OF "MOTHER" AND OTHER STORIES, Mary E. Wilkins Freeman. 128pp. 40428-5 $1.50

MADAME BOVARY, Gustave Flaubert. 256pp. 29257-6 $2.00

WHERE ANGELS FEAR TO TREAD, E. M. Forster. 128pp. (Available in U.S. only.) 27791-7 $1.50

A ROOM WITH A VIEW, E. M. Forster. 176pp. (Available in U.S. only.) 28467-0 $2.00

THE IMMORALIST, André Gide. 112pp. (Available in U.S. only.) 29237-1 $1.50

"THE YELLOW WALLPAPER" AND OTHER STORIES, Charlotte Perkins Gilman. 80pp. 29857-4 $1.00

HERLAND, Charlotte Perkins Gilman. 128pp. 40429-3 $1.50

THE OVERCOAT AND OTHER STORIES, Nikolai Gogol. 112pp. 27057-2 $1.50

GREAT GHOST STORIES, John Grafton (ed.). 112pp. 27270-2 $1.00

DETECTION BY GASLIGHT, Douglas G. Greene (ed.). 272pp. 29928-7 $2.00

THE MABINOGION, Lady Charlotte E. Guest. 192pp. 29541-9 $2.00

"THE FIDDLER OF THE REELS" AND OTHER SHORT STORIES, Thomas Hardy. 80pp. 29960-0 $1.50

THE LUCK OF ROARING CAMP AND OTHER STORIES, Bret Harte. 96pp. 27271-0 $1.00

THE SCARLET LETTER, Nathaniel Hawthorne. 192pp. 28048-9 $2.00

YOUNG GOODMAN BROWN AND OTHER STORIES, Nathaniel Hawthorne. 128pp. 27060-2 $1.00

THE GIFT OF THE MAGI AND OTHER SHORT STORIES, O. Henry. 96pp. 27061-0 $1.00

THE NUTCRACKER AND THE GOLDEN POT, E. T. A. Hoffmann. 128pp. 27806-9 $1.00

THE BEAST IN THE JUNGLE AND OTHER STORIES, Henry James. 128pp. 27552-3 $1.50

DAISY MILLER, Henry James. 64pp. 28773-4 $1.00

THE TURN OF THE SCREW, Henry James. 96pp. 26684-2 $1.00

WASHINGTON SQUARE, Henry James. 176pp. 40431-5 $2.00

THE COUNTRY OF THE POINTED FIRS, Sarah Orne Jewett. 96pp. 28196-5 $1.00

THE AUTOBIOGRAPHY OF AN EX-COLORED MAN, James Weldon Johnson. 112pp. 28512-X $1.00

DUBLINERS, James Joyce. 160pp. 26870-5 $1.00

A PORTRAIT OF THE ARTIST AS A YOUNG MAN, James Joyce. 192pp. 28050-0 $2.00

THE METAMORPHOSIS AND OTHER STORIES, Franz Kafka. 96pp. 29030-1 $1.50

THE MAN WHO WOULD BE KING AND OTHER STORIES, Rudyard Kipling. 128pp. 28051-9 $1.50

YOU KNOW ME AL, Ring Lardner. 128pp. 28513-8 $1.50

SELECTED SHORT STORIES, D. H. Lawrence. 128pp. 27794-1 $1.50

GREEN TEA AND OTHER GHOST STORIES, J. Sheridan LeFanu. 96pp. 27795-X $1.50

SHORT STORIES, Theodore Dreiser. 112pp. 28215-5 $1.50

THE CALL OF THE WILD, Jack London. 64pp. 26472-6 $1.00

FIVE GREAT SHORT STORIES, Jack London. 96pp. 27063-7 $1.00

WHITE FANG, Jack London. 160pp. 26968-X $1.00

DEATH IN VENICE, Thomas Mann. 96pp. (Available in U.S. only.) 28714-9 $1.00

IN A GERMAN PENSION: 13 Stories, Katherine Mansfield. 112pp. 28719-X $1.50

THE MOON AND SIXPENCE, W. Somerset Maugham. 176pp. (Available in U.S. only.) 28731-9 $2.00

DOVER · THRIFT · EDITIONS

FICTION

THE NECKLACE AND OTHER SHORT STORIES, Guy de Maupassant. 128pp. 27064-5 $1.00

BARTLEBY AND BENITO CERENO, Herman Melville. 112pp. 26473-4 $1.00

THE OIL JAR AND OTHER STORIES, Luigi Pirandello. 96pp. 28459-X $1.00

THE GOLD-BUG AND OTHER TALES, Edgar Allan Poe. 128pp. 26875-6 $1.00

TALES OF TERROR AND DETECTION, Edgar Allan Poe. 96pp. 28744-0 $1.00

THE QUEEN OF SPADES AND OTHER STORIES, Alexander Pushkin. 128pp. 28054-3 $1.50

SREDNI VASHTAR AND OTHER STORIES, Saki (H. H. Munro). 96pp. 28521-9 $1.00

THE STORY OF AN AFRICAN FARM, Olive Schreiner. 256pp. 40165-0 $2.00

FRANKENSTEIN, Mary Shelley. 176pp. 28211-2 $1.00

THREE LIVES, Gertrude Stein. 176pp. (Available in U.S. only.) 28059-4 $2.00

THE STRANGE CASE OF DR. JEKYLL AND MR. HYDE, Robert Louis Stevenson. 64pp. 26688-5 $1.00

TREASURE ISLAND, Robert Louis Stevenson. 160pp. 27559-0 $1.50

GULLIVER'S TRAVELS, Jonathan Swift. 240pp. 29273-8 $2.00

THE KREUTZER SONATA AND OTHER SHORT STORIES, Leo Tolstoy. 144pp. 27805-0 $1.50

THE WARDEN, Anthony Trollope. 176pp. 40076-X $2.00

FIRST LOVE AND DIARY OF A SUPERFLUOUS MAN, Ivan Turgenev. 96pp. 28775-0 $1.50

FATHERS AND SONS, Ivan Turgenev. 176pp. 40073-5 $2.00

ADVENTURES OF HUCKLEBERRY FINN, Mark Twain. 224pp. 28061-6 $2.00

THE ADVENTURES OF TOM SAWYER, Mark Twain. 192pp. 40077-8 $2.00

THE MYSTERIOUS STRANGER AND OTHER STORIES, Mark Twain. 128pp. 27069-6 $1.00

HUMOROUS STORIES AND SKETCHES, Mark Twain. 80pp. 29279-7 $1.00

CANDIDE, Voltaire (François-Marie Arouet). 112pp. 26689-3 $1.00

GREAT SHORT STORIES BY AMERICAN WOMEN, Candace Ward (ed.). 192pp. 28776-9 $2.00

"THE COUNTRY OF THE BLIND" AND OTHER SCIENCE-FICTION STORIES, H. G. Wells. 160pp. (Available in U.S. only.) 29569-9 $1.00

THE ISLAND OF DR. MOREAU, H. G. Wells. 112pp. (Available in U.S. only.) 29027-1 $1.50

THE INVISIBLE MAN, H. G. Wells. 112pp. (Available in U.S. only.) 27071-8 $1.00

THE TIME MACHINE, H. G. Wells. 80pp. (Available in U.S. only.) 28472-7 $1.00

THE WAR OF THE WORLDS, H. G. Wells. 160pp. (Available in U.S. only.) 29506-0 $1.00

ETHAN FROME, Edith Wharton. 96pp. 26690-7 $1.00

SHORT STORIES, Edith Wharton. 128pp. 28235-X $1.50

THE AGE OF INNOCENCE, Edith Wharton. 288pp. 29803-5 $2.00

THE PICTURE OF DORIAN GRAY, Oscar Wilde. 192pp. 27807-7 $1.50

JACOB'S ROOM, Virginia Woolf. 144pp. (Available in U.S. only.) 40109-X $1.50

MONDAY OR TUESDAY: Eight Stories, Virginia Woolf. 64pp. (Available in U.S. only.) 29453-6 $1.00

NONFICTION

POETICS, Aristotle. 64pp. 29577-X $1.00

NICOMACHEAN ETHICS, Aristotle. 256pp. 40096-4 $2.00

MEDITATIONS, Marcus Aurelius. 128pp. 29823-X $1.50

THE LAND OF LITTLE RAIN, Mary Austin. 96pp. 29037-9 $1.50

THE DEVIL'S DICTIONARY, Ambrose Bierce. 144pp. 27542-6 $1.00

THE ANALECTS, Confucius. 128pp. 28484-0 $2.00

CONFESSIONS OF AN ENGLISH OPIUM EATER, Thomas De Quincey. 80pp. 28742-4 $1.00

NARRATIVE OF THE LIFE OF FREDERICK DOUGLASS, Frederick Douglass. 96pp. 28499-9 $1.00

DOVER · THRIFT · EDITIONS

NONFICTION

THE SOULS OF BLACK FOLK, W. E. B. Du Bois. 176pp. 28041-1 $2.00

SELF-RELIANCE AND OTHER ESSAYS, Ralph Waldo Emerson. 128pp. 27790-9 $1.00

THE LIFE OF OLAUDAH EQUIANO, OR GUSTAVUS VASSA, THE AFRICAN, Olaudah Equiano. 192pp. 40661-X $2.00

THE AUTOBIOGRAPHY OF BENJAMIN FRANKLIN, Benjamin Franklin. 144pp. 29073-5 $1.50

TOTEM AND TABOO, Sigmund Freud. 176pp. (Available in U.S. only.) 40434-X $2.00

LOVE: A Book of Quotations, Herb Galewitz (ed.). 64pp. 40004-2 $1.00

PRAGMATISM, William James. 128pp. 28270-8 $1.50

THE STORY OF MY LIFE, Helen Keller. 80pp. 29249-5 $1.00

TAO TE CHING, Lao Tze. 112pp. 29792-6 $1.00

GREAT SPEECHES, Abraham Lincoln. 112pp. 26872-1 $1.00

THE PRINCE, Niccolò Machiavelli. 80pp. 27274-5 $1.00

THE SUBJECTION OF WOMEN, John Stuart Mill. 112pp. 29601-6 $1.50

SELECTED ESSAYS, Michel de Montaigne. 96pp. 29109-X $1.50

UTOPIA, Sir Thomas More. 96pp. 29583-4 $1.50

BEYOND GOOD AND EVIL: Prelude to a Philosophy of the Future, Friedrich Nietzsche. 176pp. 29868-X $1.50

THE BIRTH OF TRAGEDY, Friedrich Nietzsche. 96pp. 28515-4 $1.50

COMMON SENSE, Thomas Paine. 64pp. 29602-4 $1.00

SYMPOSIUM AND PHAEDRUS, Plato. 96pp. 27798-4 $1.50

THE TRIAL AND DEATH OF SOCRATES: Four Dialogues, Plato. 128pp. 27066-1 $1.00

A MODEST PROPOSAL AND OTHER SATIRICAL WORKS, Jonathan Swift. 64pp. 28759-9 $1.00

CIVIL DISOBEDIENCE AND OTHER ESSAYS, Henry David Thoreau. 96pp. 27563-9 $1.00

SELECTIONS FROM THE JOURNALS (Edited by Walter Harding), Henry David Thoreau. 96pp. 28760-2 $1.00

WALDEN; OR, LIFE IN THE WOODS, Henry David Thoreau. 224pp. 28495-6 $2.00

NARRATIVE OF SOJOURNER TRUTH, Sojourner Truth. 80pp. 29899-X $1.00

THE THEORY OF THE LEISURE CLASS, Thorstein Veblen. 256pp. 28062-4 $2.50

DE PROFUNDIS, Oscar Wilde. 64pp. 29308-4 $1.00

OSCAR WILDE'S WIT AND WISDOM: A Book of Quotations, Oscar Wilde. 64pp. 40146-4 $1.00

UP FROM SLAVERY, Booker T. Washington. 160pp. 28738-6 $2.00

A VINDICATION OF THE RIGHTS OF WOMAN, Mary Wollstonecraft. 224pp. 29036-0 $2.00

PLAYS

PROMETHEUS BOUND, Aeschylus. 64pp. 28762-9 $1.00

THE ORESTEIA TRILOGY: Agamemnon, The Libation-Bearers and The Furies, Aeschylus. 160pp. 29242-8 $1.50

LYSISTRATA, Aristophanes. 64pp. 28225-2 $1.00

WHAT EVERY WOMAN KNOWS, James Barrie. 80pp. (Available in U.S. only.) 29578-8 $1.50

THE CHERRY ORCHARD, Anton Chekhov. 64pp. 26682-6 $1.00

THE SEA GULL, Anton Chekhov. 64pp. 40656-3 $1.50

THE THREE SISTERS, Anton Chekhov. 64pp. 27544-2 $1.50

UNCLE VANYA, Anton Chekhov. 64pp. 40159-6 $1.50

THE WAY OF THE WORLD, William Congreve. 80pp. 27787-9 $1.50

BACCHAE, Euripides. 64pp. 29580-X $1.00

MEDEA, Euripides. 64pp. 27548-5 $1.00

THE MIKADO, William Schwenck Gilbert. 64pp. 27268-0 $1.50

DOVER·THRIFT·EDITIONS

PLAYS